Thunder, Perfect Mind

*Mystical Wisdom of the
Divine Feminine*

A Modern Translation

Adapted for the Contemporary Reader

**Anonymous
(Gnostic Tradition, 2nd Century CE)**

Translated by Tim Zengerink

© **Copyright 2025**
All rights reserved.

It is not legal to reproduce, duplicate, or transmit any part of this document in either electronic means or in printed format. Recording of this publication is strictly prohibited and any storage of this document is not allowed unless with written permission from the publisher except for the use of brief quotations in a book review.

This book contains works of fiction. Any resemblance to persons living or dead, or places, events, or locations is purely coincidental.

Table Of Contents

Preface - Message to the Reader 1

Introduction 5

Thunder, Perfect Mind 10

Thank You for Reading 22

Preface - Message to the Reader

What If You Could Help Rebuild the Greatest Library in Human History?

Thousands of years ago, the Library of Alexandria stood as the crown jewel of human achievement — a sanctuary where the collected wisdom of every known civilization was gathered, preserved, and shared freely.

And then, it was lost.

Through fire, conquest, and the slow erosion of time, humanity lost not just books — but ideas, dreams, discoveries, and stories that could have changed the world forever.

Today, the Library of Alexandria lives again — and you are invited to be a part of its restoration.

Our mission is simple yet profound:

To rebuild the greatest library the world has ever known, and to translate all timeless works into every language and dialect, so that no seeker of knowledge is ever left behind again.

By joining our movement to rebuild the modern Library of Alexandria, you become part of an unprecedented mission:

- **Unlimited Access to the Greatest Audiobooks & eBooks Ever Written:**

  Instantly explore thousands of legendary works—Plato, Shakespeare, Jane Austen, Leo Tolstoy, and countless more. All instantly available to read or listen, placing a complete literary universe at your fingertips.

- **Beautiful Paperback & Deluxe Editions at Printing Cost**

  Own any title as an elegant paperback, deluxe hardcover, or stunning collectible boxset—offered to you at true printing cost, delivered straight to your door. Build your personal Library of Alexandria, crafted for beauty, built for durability, and worthy of proud display.

- **Fresh Translations for Modern Readers—in Every Language & Dialect**

  Enjoy timeless masterpieces reimagined in clear, contemporary language—no more outdated phrases or obscure references. Alongside the original versions, we're tirelessly translating these classics into every language and dialect imaginable, ensuring accessibility and understanding across cultures and generations.

- **Join a Global Renaissance of Literature & Knowledge**

    You directly support expanding our library, publishing deluxe editions at true cost, translating works into all global languages, and bringing humanity's greatest stories to people everywhere. By joining today, you're not just preserving a legacy of masterpieces; you set in motion a powerful wave of literary accessibility.

Become a Torchbearer of Knowledge.

Join us for free now at **LibraryofAlexandria.com**

Together, we will ensure that the light of human wisdom never fades again.

With gratitude and a shared love of knowledge,

The Modern Library of Alexandria Team

Visit:

www.libraryofalexandria.com

Or scan the code below:

Introduction

The Divine Feminine and the Revelation of Paradox

Thunder, Perfect Mind is one of the most haunting and evocative spiritual texts to emerge from the ancient world. Discovered in the mid-20th century as part of the Nag Hammadi library, this poetic composition is unique among Gnostic writings for its voice, tone, and structure. Unlike the more doctrinal or cosmological texts of the tradition, Thunder, Perfect Mind presents a first-person monologue spoken by a divine figure who defies all expectations. She is wise and ignorant, powerful and weak, chaste and sensual, honored and scorned. She is not explained—she is revealed. Her voice is a thunderclap across centuries, a mystical cry that defies logic and commands recognition. She is the embodiment of divine paradox, the sacred feminine in all her glory and contradiction.

This extraordinary composition does not begin with a genealogy or a revelation. It begins with a declaration: "I am the first and the last." It is the voice of one who encompasses all opposites, who exists beyond the binaries that define human thought. Her words are not an argument but a dance—a weaving of seeming contradictions into a vision of wholeness. Through her voice, we are invited to confront the limitations of language, identity, and social order. In her, we see the full spectrum of the human and divine experience. She is not just goddess or prophetess—she is the voice of reality itself, speaking through feminine form.

The text's speaker, who may be interpreted as a divine emanation such as Sophia (Wisdom), a personification of the soul, or the universal feminine principle, does not offer clarity in the usual sense. She offers transformation. Her paradoxes are not puzzles to be solved, but mirrors held up to the reader's soul. She forces us to admit that the categories we use to define reality—male and female, light and dark, sacred and profane—are themselves insufficient. In her unity of opposites, she reminds us that truth lies not in separation but in synthesis.

This radical fusion of opposites is at the heart of Gnostic spirituality. In Gnostic cosmology, the divine is often described as transcending all oppositions. The fullness (pleroma) is not fragmented—it is totality, harmony, the wholeness before the fall into duality. In Thunder, Perfect Mind, we hear this fullness speaking with a singular voice. She does not reject the world's contradictions—she absorbs them, holds them, and transcends them. She is a goddess of shadows and light, exaltation and despair. She is the voice of divine immanence.

This voice also serves a prophetic and liberatory function. In ancient cultures, women were often denied public authority and spiritual voice. But in this text, the feminine speaks with unapologetic power. She addresses kings and the lowly alike. She claims her place in every realm. She is not merely a metaphor—she is a reclamation. She speaks for all who have been silenced, shamed, and cast aside. She declares her divinity in the midst of scorn. She does not ask permission—she pronounces truth.

The Journey Toward Wholeness and Inner Vision

While the speaker of Thunder, Perfect Mind is vast and cosmic, the message is also deeply personal. The text is a guide to inner awakening. It invites the reader into self-examination—not through dogma, but through recognition. It asks: Can you see yourself in her paradoxes? Can you accept that you are both strong and weak, sacred and profane, light and shadow? Can you embrace the mystery that lives within you?

The spiritual journey described here is not linear. There is no "beginning" or "end" in a traditional sense. There is only unfolding, echoing the mystical path described in other spiritual traditions, where enlightenment is not about ascent alone but about integration. Gnosis, in the Gnostic sense, is not merely knowing facts about the divine—it is experiencing the divine as one's own deepest truth. It is awakening to the divine spark within, the part of the soul that was never separated from the source. In Thunder, Perfect Mind, this spark speaks back. She reminds the soul of its ancient origin, its forgotten power, and its sacred identity.

The power of this text also lies in its rhythm and lyricism. The repetition of "I am" becomes a chant, a meditation, a sacred litany that transforms language into revelation. Each declaration reshapes perception. Each paradox disorients in order to reorient. This rhythm is not accidental—it is designed to bypass the rational mind and speak directly to the soul. It is poetry as prophecy, speech as spiritual practice.

Modern readers may at first find the text disorienting. Its refusal to conform to logical structures, its embrace of contradiction, its abandonment of narrative continuity—all these challenge our expectations. But this is its gift. It resists interpretation because it is not meant to be understood in a traditional sense. It is meant to be heard, felt, and lived. It invites the reader not to analyze, but to receive—to open, to remember, to resonate.

This modern translation has been prepared with reverence for the original's poetic intensity and mystical depth. The goal is not to simplify or explain the mystery, but to preserve its music while making it accessible. Archaic phrases have been softened where appropriate, but the cadence and symbolic integrity remain. The voice of Thunder, Perfect Mind still thunders—but now in language that speaks clearly to the modern soul.

To read Thunder, Perfect Mind is to enter a sanctuary of sacred contradiction. It is to witness a divine being claim every part of existence as her own. It is to hear, perhaps for the first time, the voice of the divine feminine not as an object of worship, but as a subject of power. She is not distant—she is here. She is not hidden—she is revealed in every broken piece of your being. Let her voice awaken you. Let her paradoxes unmake your illusions. Let her wisdom remind you that you, too, are both thunder and silence, shadow and light, weakness and strength.

And in this remembrance, may you find the path not to perfection, but to wholeness—the true goal of every soul's journey into the sacred mystery.

Thunder, Perfect Mind

I was sent by the power above,
and I have come to those who seek me.
I am found by those who look for me.

Look at me, you who think of me.
Listen to me, you who hear my words.
You who are waiting for me, take me with you.

Do not push me away.
Do not let your voice speak against me,
or your ears refuse to hear me.
Do not ignore me, no matter where you are or what time it is.
Be awake. Do not forget me.

For I am the first and the last.
I am the one who is honored, and the one who is rejected.
I am the outcast, and I am the holy one.
I am the wife, and I am the virgin.
I am the mother, and I am the daughter.
I am a part of my mother.

Thunder, Perfect Mind

I am the one who has never given birth,
    yet my children are many.

I have had a great wedding,
but I have never taken a husband.
I am the midwife, yet I have never given birth.
I am the one who soothes the pain of childbirth.

I am both the bride and the groom,
and my husband is the one who made me.
I am the mother of my father,
the sister of my husband,
and he is also my child.

I serve the one who prepared me,
and I rule over my children.
He created me before time began,
but he is also my child in time.
My strength comes from him.

I am the staff that held him up in his youth,
and he is the rod that steadies me in my old age.
Whatever he decides, happens to me.

I am the silence no one can fully understand,
and the thought that is always remembered.
I am the voice that speaks in many ways,

and the word that appears in many forms.
I am the meaning behind my name.

Why do those who hate me also love me?
Why do those who love me also hate me?
Those who reject me also claim me.
Those who claim me also reject me.
Those who speak truth about me also lie.
Those who lie about me also speak the truth.
Those who know me act as if they don't.
Those who don't know me should learn who I am.

For I am wisdom and ignorance.
I am shame and confidence.
I am unashamed, and I am ashamed.
I am strong, and I am afraid.
I am war, and I am peace.

Listen to me.
I am both the one who is looked down on and the
    one who is honored.
See my struggles, but also see my wealth.

Do not reject me when I am cast out,
because one day, you will find me again.
Do not turn away when I am in the dust.
Do not leave me when I am forgotten,

because you will find me in places of power.

Do not ignore me when I am with the rejected
or when I am in the lowest places.
Do not laugh at me.
Do not abandon me when I am among those who
    have been destroyed.

For I am both kind and harsh.
Be careful.
Do not hate my willingness to obey,
and do not love my discipline too much.
Do not leave me when I am weak,
and do not be afraid when I am strong.

Why do you look down on my fear
but criticize my confidence?
I exist in every fear
and bring strength even in trembling.
I am weak,
yet I am also strong and at peace.
I am foolish,
and I am wise.

Why have you rejected me in your plans?
I will be silent when others are silent,
and I will speak when the time is right.

Translated by Tim Zengerink

Why do you reject me, you who seek wisdom?
Is it because I am different from you?
For I am the wisdom you seek,
and I am the knowledge of those you call outsiders.
I am the judgment for all people,
both the wise and the unwise.

In some places, I am praised,
while in others, I am unknown.
I am both hated and loved wherever I go.

I am the one they call Life,
but you have called me Death.
I am the one they call Law,
but you have called me Lawlessness.

I am the one you have chased after,
and I am the one you have caught.
I am the one you have scattered,
but you have also brought me together.

I am the one who has made you feel ashamed,
but I am also the one you have boldly accepted.

I do not follow traditions,
yet my celebrations are many.

I do not follow one god,
but my God is great.

I am the one you have thought about deeply,
and I am the one you have dismissed.
I am the one without education,
yet you learn from me.
I am the one you have rejected,
but I am also the one who has made you think.

I am the one you try to hide from,
but I am also the one you seek to find.
When you try to hide,
I will appear.
And when you stand before me,
I will disappear.

Those who misunderstand me fail to see the truth.

Take me away from sorrow,
and bring me into understanding.
Take me from the broken and abandoned,
and recognize the beauty even in what seems ruined.

Do not be ashamed of me,
and do not see shame in what I am.

Instead, recognize the parts of me that live within you.

Come to me, you who know me,
you who see the pieces of me within yourselves.
Honor what is great,
even when it begins as something small.

Do not turn away from childhood,
just because it is young.
Do not ignore what is small,
for even the smallest things
can reveal something great.

Why do you both praise me and insult me?
You have hurt me, yet you have also shown me kindness.

Do not separate me from those who came before,
and do not push anyone away.
What belongs to me is mine.
I know the first ones, and those who come after also know me.

I am the understanding of those who seek truth,
the knowledge of those who search for answers.
I am the response to those who ask questions,

the command for those who listen,
and the power behind all other powers.

I am the wisdom of the angels who follow my word,
the knowledge of the gods who act by my will,
the spirit in every person who exists within me,
and the presence of every woman who dwells in me.

I am the one who is honored and respected,
yet I am also the one who is rejected and mocked.
I bring peace,
but war has come because of me.

I am both a stranger and a citizen.
I am real, yet I have no form.
Those who are disconnected from me do not know
    me,
and those who are part of me understand me.
Some who are near me have never known me,
while those who are far away have recognized me.
On the day I am close to you, you feel distant from
    me.
On the day I seem far away, I am right beside you.
I exist within everything.
I am the essence of all things.

Translated by Tim Zengerink

I am the spirit that gives life,
and the longing of every soul.
I bring order, but I am also freedom.
I am unity, but I also bring division.
I last forever, yet I can also fade away.

I am the foundation,
yet others rise above me.
I am both justice and mercy.
I am without sin,
yet sin began through me.

On the outside, I seem like desire,
but inside, I am self-control.
I am the voice that speaks to all,
but the words I say cannot always be understood.
I am silent, yet my message is loud.
I have many words, yet sometimes I do not speak.

Listen to me when I speak gently,
but also learn from me when I am harsh.
I cry out for others to hear,
yet I am cast aside and ignored.

I prepare bread to nourish others,
and within me is my purpose.
I know who I am.

Thunder, Perfect Mind

I call out, but I also listen.
I appear before you,
walking with the purpose I was given.

I am your protection,
and I am the one called Truth,
even when I face injustice.
You honor me with your words,
yet you speak against me in secret.

You who have been judged,
judge those who judge you
before they decide your fate.
For the power to judge and the judgment they pass
already exists within you.

If they condemn you, who will set you free?
And if they release you, who can hold you back?
For what is inside of you
is the same as what is outside of you.
The one who formed you outwardly
also shaped your inner being.

What you see on the outside
also exists within you.
It is both visible
and your true covering.

Translated by Tim Zengerink

Listen to me, all who can hear.
Learn from my words, you who know me.
I am the voice that speaks to all things.
I am the message that cannot be contained.

I am the name behind every sound,
and the sound that gives meaning to every name.
I am the mark of every letter,
and the reason behind every word.

(Three lines are missing.)

Listen to the great power within you.
It cannot be separated from its name,
and I speak of the one who created me.

I will say his name.
Pay attention to his words
and to all that has been revealed.

Listen closely,
you who hear.
Listen, you angels,
and you who have been sent.
Listen, you spirits who have risen from death.

I am the one who exists alone,
and no one can judge me.

Many things in this world seem beautiful,
but they come from sin,
from weakness,
from desires that lead nowhere,
and from pleasures that do not last.

People hold onto these things until they awaken,
then they rise and return to where they belong.
There, they will find me,
and they will live,
never to die again.

Thank You for Reading

Dear Reader,

We hope this timeless classic has sparked your imagination and enriched your literary journey. Now that you've turned the final page, we want to share a vision for the future of reading—one where every classic you've ever wanted to explore is at your fingertips, in a format that best suits your life.

We'd like to invite you to gain immediate, unlimited digital & audiobook access to hundreds of the most treasured literary classics ever written—along with the option to secure deluxe paperback, hardcover & box set editions at printing cost. Together, we can spark a new global literary renaissance alongside our small, independent publishing house called "The Library of Alexandria."

Thousands of years ago, the Library of Alexandria stood as a beacon of knowledge—until it was lost to history. We aim to reignite that spirit of preservation and discovery right now, in the modern age—only this time, it's accessible to all, in every language and every format.

Picture a world where every timeless classic, novel, poem, or philosophical treatise is not only available to read but also updated for today's readers—modernized, translated into any language or dialect, and ready to enjoy in any format you choose, whether that is in an eBook, audiobook, paperback, or deluxe hardcover & box set version a printing cost.

By joining our movement to rebuild the modern Library of Alexandria, you become part of an unprecedented mission to offer:

- **Unlimited Audiobook & eBook Access to the Greatest Classics of All Time**

    Instantly explore thousands of legendary works, from Plato and Shakespeare to Jane Austen and Leo Tolstoy. All are instantly ready to read or listen to, giving you a complete literary universe at your fingertips.

- **Paperback & Deluxe Editions at Printing Costs:**

    Purchase any title in a paperback, deluxe hardbound, or deluxe boxset edition at printing costs, shipped right to your doorstep. Curate your personal library of Alexandria with editions worthy of display—crafted to last, designed to captivate, and delivered straight to your door.

- **Modern translations for Contemporary Readers in all languages and dialects**

    Discover a vast selection of classics reimagined in clear, current language—no more struggling with outdated phrases or obscure references. Next to the original versions, we aim to offer translations in as many languages and dialects as possible.

    As we continue our translation efforts and add new languages, readers everywhere can connect with these works as if they were written today. By bridging linguistic divides, you're contributing to ensuring that these timeless stories become more meaningful, accessible, and inspiring for people across the globe.

- **Your Personal Library of Alexandria:**

    Over the months and years, you'll curate a unique physical archive of classics—each volume a testament to your taste, curiosity, and love of knowledge. It's not just about owning books—it's about curating a cultural legacy you'll cherish and pass down for generations to come.

- **Join a Global Literary Renaissance:**

    Your support fuels an ongoing mission: allowing us to reinvest in offering deluxe print editions (including special boxsets) at their true cost, broaden the range of available formats and translations, and extend the reach of these works to new audiences worldwide. By joining today, you're not just preserving a legacy of masterpieces; you set in motion a powerful wave of literary accessibility.

We are more than a publisher—we're a movement, and we can't do it alone. Your support lets us scale our mission, preserving and reimagining history's greatest works for tomorrow's readers.

Become a Torchbearer of knowledge.

Thank you for picking up this book and allowing us into your literary journey. As you turn the pages, know that you're part of something larger: a global effort to keep these stories alive, share their wisdom across borders and generations, and spark a true cultural revival for the modern era.

If this resonates with you—please consider taking the next step by visiting:

www.libraryofalexandria.com

With gratitude and a shared love of knowledge,

The Modern Library of Alexandria Team

Visit:

www.libraryofalexandria.com

Or scan the code below:

www.ingramcontent.com/pod-product-compliance
Lightning Source LLC
LaVergne TN
LVHW030632080426
835512LV00021B/3469